D0745897

LIFE'S LITTLE
TREASURE BOOK

On Wisdom

H. JACKSON BROWN, JR.

RUTLEDGE HILL PRESS
NASHVILLE, TENNESSEE

Published in Nashville, Tennessee, by
Rutledge Hill Press, Inc., 211 Seventh Avenue
North, Nashville, Tennessee 37219.
Distributed in Canada by H. B. Fenn and
Company Ltd., Mississauga, Ontario.

Typography by D&T/Bailey Typesetting, Inc.,
Nashville, Tennessee
Illustrations by Cristine Mortensen
Book design by Harriette Bateman

ISBN: 1-55853-279-X

Printed in Hong Kong through Palace Press
1 2 3 4 5 6 7 8 9 — 97 96 95 94

INTRODUCTION

I once read that you can inherit wealth but never wisdom. Wisdom, for most of us, is acquired in the thicket of experience. If we live long enough, wisdom usually meets us somewhere along the way. But like an Iowa farmer advised, the trick is to get wise before you get old.

I shared what I knew about wisdom with my son, Adam, in the

two volumes of *Life's Little Instruction Book*. This book contains many of those observations and discoveries. As you read them you'll discover a common thread, for the truly wise among us know that wisdom is based on the development of good character and adherence to the principles of honesty, self-discipline, responsibility, persistence, gratitude, and forgiveness.

But wisdom is also knowing what to ignore. An old prayer asks for the courage to change what can be changed, the serenity to accept what cannot be changed, and the wisdom to know the difference; teaching us that wisdom in its purest form is sometimes knowing what to overlook.

*B*e kinder than necessary.

∾

*L*earn to recognize the
inconsequential;
then ignore it.

∾

*E*very person that you meet
knows something you don't;
learn from them.

$\mathcal{G}$et involved with your local
government. As someone said,
"Politics is too important to be
left to the politicians."

∾

$\mathcal{W}$atch
"The Andy Griffith Show"
to help keep things
in perspective.

$\mathcal{V}$olunteer to help a few hours
a month working in a
soup kitchen.

∾

$\mathcal{D}$on't waste time responding
to your critics.

*Wisdom is the
principal thing;
therefore get wisdom.
And in all your getting,
get understanding.*

— Proverbs 4:7

$\mathcal{K}$eep a tight rein on
your temper.

∾

$\mathcal{R}$emember that the more you
know, the less you fear.

∾

$\mathcal{D}$on't expect money
to bring you happiness

*N*ever resist

a generous

impulse.

*R*esist telling people how
something should be done.
Instead, tell them what
needs to be done.
They will often surprise you
with creative solutions.

∾

*K*eep it simple.

What is the use of living if it not be to strive for noble causes and to make this muddled world a better place for those who will live in it after we are gone?

— Winston Churchill

*D*on't stop the parade
to pick up a dime.

∾

*A*void sarcastic remarks.

∾

*M*easure people by the size of
their hearts, not the size of
their bank accounts.

Never sell your teddy bear, letter sweater, or high school yearbooks at a garage sale. You'll regret it later.

*R*emember that the person
who steals an egg will
steal a chicken.

❧

*D*on't spread yourself too thin.
Learn to say no
politely and quickly.

Share your
knowledge.
It's a way to achieve
immortality.

$\mathcal{A}$ct with courtesy and fairness regardless of how others treat you.
Don't let them determine your response.

～

$\mathcal{D}$on't watch violent television shows, and don't buy the products that sponsor them.

Trust in God
but lock
your car.

$\mathcal{M}$ake the punishment
fit the crime.

❧

$\mathcal{W}$hen you're buying
something that you only
need to buy once,
buy the best
you can afford.

Show respect for everyone
who works for a living,
regardless of how
trivial their job.

∽

Keep a daily journal.

∽

Mind your own business.

Don't major
in minor things.

$\mathcal{R}$emember that what's right
isn't always popular, and
what's popular isn't
always right.

∾

$\mathcal{B}$e modest.
A lot was accomplished
before you were born.

$\mathcal{D}$on't burn bridges. You'll be
surprised how many times you
have to cross the same river.

∽

$\mathcal{W}$hen declaring your rights,
don't forget
your responsibilities.

Never swap
your integrity
for money,
power,
or fame.

$\mathcal{L}$oosen up. Relax.
Except for rare
life-and-death matters,
nothing is as important
as it first seems.

$\mathcal{E}$very so often watch
"Sesame Street."

∾

$\mathcal{N}$o matter how dire the
situation, keep your cool.

∾

$\mathcal{H}$ear both sides
before judging.

Never deprive
someone
of hope;
it might be all they
have.

*U*se your wit to amuse,
not abuse.

∾

*N*ever take action when
you're angry.

∾

*B*e tactful. Never alienate
anyone on purpose.

$\mathcal{D}$on't use time or words carelessly. Neither can be retrieved.

$\mathcal{G}$ive yourself a year
and read the Bible
cover to cover.

∽

$\mathcal{W}$hen you realize that
you've made a mistake,
take immediate steps
to correct it.

*Expect trouble as an
inevitable part of life and
repeat to yourself the most
comforting words of all:
"This, too, shall pass."*

— Ann Landers

$\mathcal{M}$ake a list of
twenty-five things you want
to experience before you die.
Carry it in your wallet and
refer to it often.

&

$\mathcal{D}$on't insist on running
someone else's life.

Think big thoughts,
but relish small pleasures.

∽

Remember that how
you say something
is as important as
what you say.

$\mathcal{R}$emember the
three Rs:
Respect for self;
Respect for others;
Responsibility for all
your actions.

For the next
twenty-four hours
refrain from criticizing
anybody or anything.

❧

Meet regularly with someone
who holds vastly different
views than you.

$\mathcal{N}$ever
underestimate
the power of a
kind word
or deed.

$\mathcal{B}$e a good loser.

◊

$\mathcal{B}$e a good winner.

◊

$\mathcal{B}$e especially
courteous and patient
with older people.

*R*emember that
a good example
is the
best sermon.

*P*ay your fair share.

∾

*D*on't miss the magic
of the moment by focusing
on what's to come.

∾

*N*ever claim a
victory prematurely.

$\mathcal{D}$o the
right thing,
regardless of
what others think.

$\mathcal{N}$ever remind someone of a
kindness or act of generosity
you have shown him or her.
Bestow a favor and
then forget it.

∾

$\mathcal{H}$ire people more for their
judgment than for their talents.

Beware of the person who
has nothing to lose.

∾

Never decide to do
nothing just because you
can only do a little.
Do what you can.

Remember that
your character is
your destiny.

Stand at attention and put your hand over your heart when singing the national anthem.

∿

Contribute 5 percent of your income to charity.

Never underestimate
your power to
change yourself.

∾

Never overestimate
your power to
change others.

∾

Respect tradition.

$\mathcal{N}$ever apologize for
extreme measures when
defending your values,
your health, or
your family's safety.

Never be ashamed of
honest tears.

∾

Never be ashamed of
your patriotism.

∾

Be humble and polite,
but don't let anyone
push you around.

Never give up
on anybody.
Miracles happen
every day.

$\mathcal{L}$ive a good, honorable life.
Then when you get older
and think back,
you'll get to enjoy it
a second time.

∾

$\mathcal{L}$et people know
what you stand for — and
what you won't stand for.

Choose a job you love,
and you will never have to
work a day in your life.

— Confucius

*E*valuate yourself by
your own standards,
not someone else's.

❧

*R*emember that everyone you
meet wears an invisible sign.
It reads, "Notice me.
Make me feel important."

$\mathcal{D}$on't allow self-pity.
The moment this emotion
strikes, do something nice
for someone less fortunate
than you.

∾

$\mathcal{A}$pologize immediately
when you lose your temper,
especially to children.

$\mathcal{B}$e gentle
with the Earth.

*C*hoose a charity in
your community and
support it generously with
your time and money.

∾

*B*e wary of people
who tell you how
honest they are.

$\mathcal{N}$ever take what
you cannot use.

❧

$\mathcal{W}$orry makes for a hard pillow.
When something's troubling
you, before going to sleep,
jot down three things
you can do the next day to
help solve the problem.

Spend your life
lifting people up,
not putting
people down.

$\mathscr{D}$on't be fooled.
If something sounds
too good to be true,
it probably is.

∾

$\mathscr{A}$void negative people.

∾

$\mathscr{R}$egardless of the situation,
react with class.

$\mathcal{R}$eject and condemn
prejudice based on race,
gender, religion,
or age.

∾

$\mathcal{R}$emember that not
getting what you want
is sometimes a stroke
of good luck.

$\mathcal{B}$e bold and courageous.
When you look back on
your life, you'll regret
the things you didn't do
more than the ones
you did.

Remember this statement by
Coach Lou Holtz,
"Life is 10 percent what
happens to me and
90 percent how
I react to it."

∾

Don't expect life
to be fair.

*The young men know
the rules.
The old men know
the exceptions.*

—Oliver Wendell Holmes

*W*in without boasting.

∾

*L*ose without excuses.

∾

*D*on't dismiss a
good idea simply because
you don't like the source.

*P*ray.
There is
immeasurable power
in it.

*A*lways put something
in the collection plate.

∾

*W*hen you lose,
don't lose the lesson.

When you have the choice of
two exciting things,
choose the one you
haven't tried.

❧

Learn to disagree without
being disagreeable.

$\mathcal{A}$ccept a breath mint if someone offers you one.

∾

$\mathcal{M}$ake the best of bad situations.

∾

$\mathcal{D}$on't carry a grudge.

Be brave.
Even if you're not,
pretend to be.
No one can tell
the difference.

$\mathcal{D}$on't let weeds
grow around
your dreams.

Show extra respect for
people whose jobs put dirt
under their fingernails.

❧

Never threaten if you don't
intend to back it up.

❧

Don't be deceived
by first impressions.

$\mathcal{D}$on't believe all you hear,
spend all you have, or
sleep all you want.

∿

$\mathcal{D}$on't confuse comfort
with happiness.

∿

$\mathcal{D}$on't confuse foolishness
with bravery.

Be an original.
If that means
being a little
eccentric,
so be it.

Truth is serious business.
When criticizing others,
remember that a little goes
a long way.

❧

Accept the fact that
regardless of how many times
you are right,
you will sometimes
be wrong.

$\mathcal{G}$ive people a second chance,
but not a third.

∾

$\mathcal{A}$dmit your mistakes.

∾

$\mathcal{R}$emember that all
news is biased.

*B*ecome the
most positive and
enthusiastic person
you know.

*D*on't waste time
waiting for inspiration.
Begin, and inspiration will
find you.

∽

*W*hen a good man or woman
runs for political office,
support him or her with
your time and money.

$\mathcal{D}$on't say no until you've
heard the whole story.

✌

$\mathcal{R}$emember that
almost everything
looks better after a
good night's sleep.

$\mathcal{D}$on't confuse

mere inconveniences

with real

problems.

Never sell yourself short.

⌘

Never cut what can be untied.

⌘

Accept pain and
disappointment as
part of life.

*O*ur thoughts determine
our responses to life.
We are not victims
of the world.
To the extent that
we control our thoughts,
we control the world.

$\mathcal{D}$o battle against
prejudice and discrimination
wherever you find it.

❧

$\mathcal{P}$ay as much attention to
the things that are
working positively in your life
as you do to those that are
giving you trouble.

Don't go looking for trouble.

∽

Don't buy
someone else's trouble.

∽

Judge people from
where they stand,
not from where you stand.

When there is a hill to climb,
don't think that waiting
will make it smaller.

❧

Don't cut corners.

❧

Let some things remain
mysterious.

$\mathcal{H}$old yourself to the
highest standards.

∾

$\mathcal{O}$pen your arms to change,
but don't let go of
your values.

∾

$\mathcal{N}$ever ignore evil.

In business
and in family
relationships,
remember that
the most important
thing is trust.

$\mathcal{D}$on't forget that the quality of your life will be determined by the quality of the people in your life.

Never compromise
your integrity.

∽

Be tough minded
but tenderhearted.

∽

Never ask a barber
if you need a haircut.

$\mathcal{D}$on't accept
unacceptable behavior.

❧

$\mathcal{B}$e the first to fight for
a just cause.

❧

$\mathcal{L}$isten to your critics.
They will keep you
focused and innovative.

Spend less time worrying
who's right, and more time
deciding what's right.

∾

Keep your private thoughts
private.

∾

Remember that ignorance
is expensive.

*P*ray not for things,
but for wisdom and courage.

❧

*R*emember that silence is
sometimes the best answer.

❧

*D*on't mistake kindness
for weakness.